WRITING COMPELLING FICTION

Master the Fundamentals of Unforgettable Stories

WORKBOOK

NEW YORK TIMES BESTSELLING AUTHOR

SHIRLEY JUMP

Printed in the United States of America

First Printing, 2024

ISBN: 9798988677659 (paperback)

TABLE OF CONTENTS

INTRODUCTION

If you've read *Writing Compelling Fiction*, watched me on my YouTube channel, or simply come across this book because Amazon's algorithm was feeling kind, thank you. I know there's a ton of writing advice out there to choose from, which can make it confusing, frustrating, and thus, give you a *really* good excuse to procrastinate on writing the next chapter.

I love procrastination. In fact, if there were medals for Best Procrastinator, I'd be standing on the podium like an Olympian. Supposedly, Dorothy Parker once said, "I hate writing, but I love having written." Whether or not she did (we'll let Google duke that one out), most of us get paralyzed with anxiety at least once in the writing process.

For me, that point comes after the honeymoon is over, which happens around Chapter 3. For the first couple of chapters, I *LOVE* my Characters and think they are the best Characters I have ever created, this book is going to be amazing, readers are going to weep reading these scenes…

Then I get to Chapter 3 and hate everything about the book. And I realize, for the 100th time, that I need to stop leaping into the first novel relationship that comes along and actually have some kind of strategic plan in place. Listen, that kind of leap-without-looking thing doesn't work well on Tinder, and it doesn't usually work well when you're writing, either.

I'm not saying you need a General MacArthur type of battle plan with drawings and arrows and maps. You don't have to have that, but if doing that kind of planning makes your office-supply heart happy, go do that. There are no rules on how much to plan, and no one is going to come over to your house to see if you color-coordinated your plot points. Personally, I'm not that big of a planner (because I'm so busy procrastinating), so I created this workbook for people like me, those peeps who fall in the middle between Plotter and Pantser. Is that a Platter? A Plotner? A Plantser? I don't know, but I really want a T-shirt for it.

Whichever you are, this workbook is designed to allow you to plan as much as you want and to wing it as much as you want. You'll see sections labeled A Good Idea to Do, which are the ones I highly recommend you fill out, just so you have the most important elements of your book figured out before you start writing.

However, if you don't fill them out, I swear to you that the world will not collapse (and your book might not either). Skip what you want, fill in what you want, or just skim it and think about the concepts. It's your novel, not mine, so plan it your way.

There are no real rules, no real requirements, no one grading you on your penmanship (thank goodness!). All of it is entirely up to you.

In between, you'll find writing exercises to help you take your writing to the next level. There are also notes on corresponding videos that explain the concepts in this workbook. That said, my YouTube channel is an ever-evolving place where new videos are loaded every week, so chances are there will be a dozen new ones in the time it takes you to go through this book (which is why subscribing is a good idea, just sayin').

> If this feels like homework—stop doing it. There are millions of "rules" for writing but these rules are made to be broken, once you know how they work. Writing should be as fun as it is frustrating, so don't feel like you're failing at some invisible test if you skip straight to Internal Plot or only do the fun writing exercises. You do you, truly, and adapt this to meet your process.

With all of these tools, my goal is to help you write a better, stronger, more compelling novel. This companion workbook to *Writing Compelling Fiction* is just one way to help you accomplish that goal! Now let's jump right (or write, ha ha) to it!

> If you're a video learner, then check out my YouTube channel where you'll find a video for pretty much any writing topic. Throughout this workbook there are QR codes to specific videos on that section's topic. A side note: Because I'm always fiddling with my thumbnails and titles on YouTube, the ones in this book might differ from the video's current one, but don't worry, it's the same video!

THE BASICS

Let's start with the basics because they're the easy part, and I love easy parts that make me feel oh-so accomplished early in the day.

You might already know all this information, you overachiever you. If you don't, there are fun little fill-in lines for you to figure it out now. If you don't want to do this or don't know these answers, skip it and come back to fill it in later. Personally, I title my book after I get a ways into writing it, so I would skip that part but do all the others.

If you have more than two Main Characters, add some lines. If you don't have an Antagonist (you don't have to have one), just roll past that section. This is a book where it's totally cool to have some blank lines.

Later on, you'll be filling out the Plot and Character sections for each Main Character and Antagonist. Yes, you should have one for EACH Main Character and/or Antagonist. You don't need to fill these out for Secondary Characters *unless* they are going to be the Main Character in your next book (that's to help you build in the beginnings of their storyline in the first book).

For now, let's just get the basics. For me, this is like writing a To Do list that starts with "Get Out of Bed" so that I can start the day feeling accomplished before coffee.

That doesn't mean you're starting with your Main Character. Whoa, what?

No Character yet. I want to start, instead, with *you*. Why? Because you're the one writing the book and you should know what kind of writer you are before you start. Or at least have a vague idea of where you want to go…

Because the only way to carve out a path is to have a destination.

The Basics of You the Author

What kind of books do you LOVE to read? What genre? Time period? Length?

_____

_____

_____

_____

What kind of books would you LOVE to write? What genre? Time period? Length? There's a very simple reason why you need to know this—if readers love this book, they're going to want a dozen more just like it, so write what you love from day one and you'll always be writing what you love.

_____

_____

_____

_____

Do you want to write in a subgenre? For instance, you might love reading and writing historicals, but specifically love Regency historical novels. Or WWII-set novels. Maybe you love suspense, but especially love Western-set suspense. Knowing this helps you carve out your niche and what makes your stories unique.

_____

_____

_____

_____

Who is your target audience? What's their age? Demographic? What do they like to read and watch on TV? Knowing who they are can help you target the book more effectively when you are marketing it later on.

_____

_____

What kind of settings do you like to read and write? Just because small town contemporary novels are popular doesn't mean you should write them. Chasing a trend is like a dog chasing its own tail—it rarely works out for the dog. If you like dark, gritty settings or historical periods, that's what you should be writing.

What is the theme in your writing? This may be an answer you don't have yet. I know it took about seven books for me to realize I was writing about the same theme in all my books: that only by being true to who you really are (the concept in my favorite poem, *The Love Song of J. Alfred Prufrock* by T.S. Eliot) can you find happiness in your life. If you don't know your theme, no biggie. Come back to this after you've written a book or five.

What kind of voice do you have on paper? How you talk and interact with people in real life isn't necessarily how you talk and interact on the page. I'm more sarcastic on the page, a little funnier (I think), and more literary in my descriptions. Do you want to write snarky, funny books? Or ones filled with angsty choices? Ones that have a fresh, powerful voice, or ones that address social issues?

There are dozens of kinds of novels out there, which means there is room for yours. By knowing who you are as an author—and who you want to be—you can start writing the novel that best suits you. And when the novel suits you, it reads like it's coming from your heart.

> Heart = Emotional Connection and Emotional Connection = Readers who Love Your Book

A GOOD IDEA TO DO

The Basics of Your Book

Now let's move on to the basics of your book. This section, like the others that are labeled *A Good Idea to Do,* is one that will help you get your structure down. They're highly suggested, but no one is sneaking into your home office to make sure you did your homework, so you do you and you write how you want to write!

These questions are broad strokes right now; don't worry about getting too granular. There are plenty of pages ahead where you can get more specific!

Title of Your Book: _____

Main Character 1 Name: _____

Rough Description of the Character: (Age, job, marital status, etc.). _____

_____

This is known as the Dominant Impression, for those who have taken my Brainmap class (and if you haven't, no biggie because I'm going to explain it to you right now). The Dominant Impression is the way the world sees each of us, the little caption that goes beneath your face when you're interviewed on TV. It's a snapshot, essentially, of who your character is.

For example: *John Doe, 56, metalworker, divorced.*

That's who John is, what he does, and what his life status is right now. Those few words immediately form an impression in your mind, don't they? When you read *John Doe, 56, metalworker, divorced,* I bet you got a picture of our new friend John in your mind. Maybe a stereotypical image, but that's okay.

Your Character can form an immediate Dominant Impression with the reader, one that you, as the author, can turn inside out when you make your Character unique. Maybe John only welds things that are pink, or maybe he creates sculptures with his welding torch, or maybe he's a secret billionaire who welds just for fun. That's where you get to take that Dominant Impression and surprise the reader with their own misconceptions!

When you are writing this out, take a minute to think about how other Characters will interpret your Character based on this Dominant Impression. We all have prejudices and stereotypes in our heads that affect how we see others. Maybe your book will be the one to turn those prejudices and stereotypes upside down!

What is your Character's Dominant Impression?_____

_____

What perception do outsiders have of your Main Character?_____

_____

_____

Now, let's do it for any other major Characters in your book. If you don't have a second Main Character, skip this part and move on.

Main Character 2 Name: _____

Rough Description of the Character: (Age, job, marital status, etc.)._____

What perception do outsiders have of your Main Character?_____

_____

Ooh, now the Villain! Not all books have a Villain or Antagonist (just like the word implies, the Antagonist is in opposition to the Protagonist, your Main Character). If you have one, great, fill this out. If not, keep on trucking to the next section.

Villain/Antagonist Name: _____

Rough Description of the Character: (Age, job, marital status, etc.)._____

What perception do outsiders have of your Villian/Antagonist?_____

_____

Suggested Videos for More

THE WORLD BEFORE THE BOOK STARTS

I know you want to start writing about your Main Character already, and if you're burning to get to the page, don't let me stop you. However, it's pretty handy to know the life your Characters are living before the Catalyst (AKA the Trouble, AKA the Inciting Incident) happens in the book, in other words, before their life turns upside down and they need to go after their Goal.

Here's the thing: A book is about a *specific moment in time for the Main Character. A time of change and growth.* Before they start changing and growing though, you need to know their baseline.

Doing this will also tell you what the Character is risking or giving up in pursuit of the Goal, which can raise the Stakes. This might not seem like an important thing to know right now, but trust me, it is. I'll tie it all together and explain how it works, I promise.

For now, for each of the Main Characters, answer these questions:

Where is your Character at in his/her life? What are they striving for? A new job? A better relationship with a loved one? Repairing old hurts? Write a paragraph on where they are *before the book starts*. What worries they have, what concerns they have, and what is most important in their life right then.

What is their day-to-day life like? Write up a daily or weekly schedule for your Character. Do they get a cinnamon latte every Wednesday? Do they spend four hours in traffic to get to work? Do they eat pizza on Fridays? Knowing what their day-to-day life is like, who they interact with, and how their environment affects them gives you a more 3-D picture of your Character (and as the Character goes to those places in the course of the story, you have built-in histories).

_____

_____

_____

_____

_____

_____

_____

_____

_____

_____

_____

_____

Suggested Videos for More

BRILLIANT IDEAS I HAVE TO WRITE DOWN

BRILLIANT IDEAS I HAVE TO WRITE DOWN

THE CATALYST FOR CHANGE

This is one of the Good Ideas to Do because the Catalyst, AKA the Trouble, AKA the Inciting Incident, is the basis for everything in your book. It's what sets your Main Character(s) on their journey, forces them out of their comfort zone, and makes them grow and change.

You'll hear me talk about growing and changing a lot, both on the channel and in this book, because that is the core of what has to happen in your book. No matter what kind of plot you have—action-packed, or coming-of-age, or something in between—the Character must grow and change by the end of the novel.

The thing that starts them on their growing and changing journey is the Catalyst/Trouble/Inciting Incident. It's called different things by different writing teachers, but we're all referring to the same thing.

Essentially, it's the thing that gets the Character off his or her metaphorical couch and into the fray. Shrek would have never left his swamp if the fairy tale creatures hadn't been dumped there. Frodo would have never gone on that epic journey if he hadn't been saddled with the ring. The Catalyst has to be big enough to make a Character step outside their comfort zone (and give up that Ordinary World you just created for them).

That means the Catalyst has to be big and *important* to the Character. It has to threaten the Character's life, morals, status quo, relationships, or world in some way. An alien invasion is an obvious example of a Catalyst, but so too is a plane crash or a breakup.

You are asking yourself, What will make my Character act, even when the last thing they want to do is move forward? What will make my Character take risks? What will make my Character overcome their deepest fears?

A GOOD IDEA TO DO

What event changes the trajectory of your Character's life at the beginning of the book? Write that down now. Really think about this and try to make it as big and important as possible because this Catalyst *must be a catalyst for change.* Anyone who has had to make a major change in their lives (moving across the country, switching jobs, jumping off a cliff) knows there must be a big reason behind this choice, so be sure your Character has one, too.

_____

_____

_____

_____

_____

_____

_____

How is this going to impact your Character's life? What will it do to their relationships, job, home, town, etc.?

_____

_____

_____

_____

_____

_____

_____

Why is this event a BIG DEAL for your Character? It needs to be a big enough deal to force them to grow and change, so if your Catalyst won't do that, maybe come up with another one!

_____

_____

_____

_____

_____

_____

_____

Suggested Videos for More

BRILLIANT IDEAS I HAVE TO WRITE DOWN

DEEP EMOTIONAL WOUNDS

We all have Deep Emotional Wounds (DEW). We've all endured traumas that have had lasting consequences. Even if you grew up on the grounds of Disney World and had Mickey Mouse as a babysitter, you have a trauma or two. For instance, nightmares about giant mice. Seriously, though, there should be some kind of traumas in your Characters' pasts because that is what makes them believable, three-dimensional, and human.

And when they are believable, 3-D, and human, the reader can relate to them. The reader feels their pain. The reader wants to see them achieve their goal and find some kind of happy ending.

In other words, making the Characters believable, three-dimensional, and human makes readers connect. And connected readers return to your books over and over again.

The DEW also informs all of the actions and reactions your Character has. They are the traumas that create insecurities, the moments that built anxieties, the inner fears that keep them from leaping off that cliff. They are the self-imposed roadblocks that make things worse for the Character until they learn to overcome their DEW, or act in spite of them.

> Does the Deep Emotional Wound have to be some kind of massive, PTSD-generating trauma? No. Even small events can leave us with internal scars that have an emotional impact.

For example: Lindsay Lohan's character Cady Heron in *Mean Girls* has a DEW of feeling isolated and different. She hasn't fit in anywhere she's lived, and now she's the weird homeschooled girl in a school full of cool kids.

She wants so badly to fit in, rather than be ostracized or teased yet again, that she joins in on the mean girls' meanness, at the expense of her true friends.

She blows off the art show to have a party and invite the boy she's crushing on. She writes defaming remarks in the Burn Book. She doesn't stand up for the teacher who has been so kind to her.

Until Cady faces that fear inside herself and decides she's going to act in spite of it, things will spiral out of control (and they do, until the Mathathon when she embraces her inner geek). *Mean Girls* is a comedy, which means the DEW might be a little lighter than the one Jodie Foster's character has in *The Silence of the Lambs*, but there is one nonetheless.

> The Character's Deep Emotional Wounds are the driver for almost every decision and reaction they have in the story.

I want you to list a few Deep Emotional Wounds (DEWs) that your Character has. These come from events in their lives that caused some kind of emotional impact or trauma. Examples: losing his mom when he was young, being bullied when she was in middle school, fighting in a war, seeing someone die, etc.

Here's the key to this: Do not just name the event–name the *impact*. Impact is the number-one thing you must know because the impact is the base of the DEW.

For example: *Witnessing the death of his mother in a car accident has made my MC afraid to get close to anyone and to become a self-reliant loner.*

Impact is the key here—the impact on this character was that he withdrew, disconnected. How will he react to a clingy friend in the book? How will he react to a child who needs him? That's where I want your thoughts to go once you figure out the DEW. Put the Character in situations that cause them to face that DEW over and over again.

PRO TIP:

Study the Characters that you love and make a list of those Characters' DEWs. Doesn't matter if the Character is on a TV show or in a book; the point is finding the DEW. Also list the event that gave the Character that DEW and the impact of that event.

A GOOD IDEA TO DO

Creating the Deep Emotional Wounds

Why You Really, Really Should Do This: Readers who love books do so because they *bonded* with the Characters. That bond takes place when the Character is vulnerable, layered, and real. The best way to do that is to go as deep as possible emotionally with your Character. That's why I'm pretty emphatic about you doing this section of the workbook. Trust me, it'll make a huge difference in your book. Do these for your Main Character(s) and your Villian. Try to have three for each of these Main Characters.

Title of Your Book: _____

Character: _____

Event 1: _____

Impact: _____

Resulting DEW: _____

How will this impact how your Character reacts and responds? Will they fight/flee/freeze? How will it make them feel when they are confronted with something that awakens that DEW? This is super key here and makes a BIG difference in your book and its ability to emotionally connect with readers!

_____

_____

_____

_____

_____

_____

_____

Event 2: _____

Impact: _____

Resulting DEW: _____

How will this impact how your Character reacts and responds? Will they fight/flee/freeze? How will it make them feel when they are confronted with something that awakens that DEW?

_____

_____

_____

_____

_____

_____

_____

Event 3: _____

Impact: _____

Resulting DEW: _____

How will this impact how your Character reacts and responds? Will they fight/flee/freeze? How will it make them feel when they are confronted with something that awakens that DEW?

_____

_____

_____

_____

_____

_____

_____

Suggested Videos for More

BRILLIANT IDEAS I HAVE TO WRITE DOWN

THEIR WORST NIGHTMARE

This is not labeled as a Good Idea to Do because I was trying to be nice and not give you too much to do, but it is something that is pretty handy to know about your Character because it gives you a good idea of how you can torture them (on the page, ha ha). So yeah, I'd figure this out if I were you, but again, your book, your rules.

Why would you want to do this one? Because readers want to care about Characters who overcome, who work hard to achieve their goals, and when you have a Character face and conquer their Worst Nightmare, the reader is rah-rahing them the whole time.

The Worst Nightmare stems from the Deep Emotional Wound so if you are struggling to figure this out, go back to the DEW work you just did. Remember the Character whose mother died and now doesn't get close to anyone? His Worst Nightmare would be to become the sole caretaker of someone who relies completely on him and needs him 24/7, forcing him to get close.

The Worst Nightmare is the thing that the Character *least* wants to do. You may not know what your Character's Worst Nightmare is yet, but when you do, come back and fill this in. Again, look to TV and movies, and see how the Characters are forced to confront their Worst Nightmares (a woman about to get a divorce stuck in a place she can't leave with her soon-to-be-ex? First scene in Season 1 of *From*—that's the kind of Worst Nightmare I mean).

> The Character's Worst Nightmare fills your book with Conflict because the Character doesn't want to do it, but you, the mean author, are going to make the Character do it anyway to raise the Stakes and Tension in your novel.

Not only does forcing Characters to face their Worst Nightmares make the Stakes higher, it also gives them plenty of Conflict, especially Internal Conflict (we'll get to that in a second). Conflict creates Tension (*will it work out?*), and Tension keeps readers turning the pages.

Remember, people don't grow and change unless they have to, and facing your Worst Nightmare is the kind of thing that means you have to grow and change.

For example, *an agoraphobic who has to leave her house in order to catch the murderer of her child. She will overcome her fears (but it will be a battle) because achieving this Goal matters so much to her (Motivation).* We'll get deeper into Goal, Motivation, and Conflict in a second so hold on if you aren't familiar with that yet.

What is Your Character's Worst Nightmare? (Do this for each Main Character/Villain.)

How does this Worst Nightmare relate to their Deep Emotional Wounds?

How will you use this in the Plot?

_____
_____
_____
_____

What battles will your Character endure because of having to face their Worst Nightmare? In other words, what Plot events will force your Character to confront their Worst Nightmare and have to grow and change/adapt to overcome their fears?

_____
_____
_____
_____
_____
_____
_____

Suggested Videos for More

BRILLIANT IDEAS I HAVE TO WRITE DOWN

YOUR CHARACTER'S SKILLS & STRENGTHS/WEAKNESSES

These two things are great to know because you can use them to change the ending of a Scene and you can give your Character lots of depth (plus a few surprises for the reader who didn't know your Character could do that!).

While Skills and Strengths are cool, Weaknesses are even better to know because we are all our own worst enemies and are constantly self-sabotaging (eating dozens of cookies when I'm on a diet—guilty). That's a weakness that creates problems, and if my personal Scene was ending with a weigh-in at Weight Watchers, well, it wouldn't end happily (but my tummy would be happy). That's the kind of thing you want in your book. It can be as light or as deep as you want.

The most important thing about Skills & Strengths and Weaknesses: If you remember nothing else, remember this because it can transform your Scenes and Plot:

> Your Character's Weaknesses will get them into trouble over and over again in the Plot.
> However, their Skills & Strengths will save the day.

What that means is that your Character's Weaknesses (for instance, impulsiveness) will cause them to react/act a certain way (this Character might jump into a situation without thinking first and suddenly be in danger) but the Character's Skills & Strengths (maybe this Character is a great talker) save the day (this Character gets out of a deadly situation by talking the killer out of shooting, like Marty [Jason Sudeikis's Character] does in *Ozark*'s first episode). List six of each so you go a little deeper in your Character development.

Skills & Strengths:

1._____

2._____

3._____

4._____

5._____

6._____

Weaknesses:

1_____

2._____

3._____

4._____

5._____

6_____.

Hold onto these for when you start planning your Scenes. You're going to take a look at your Scene and think:

In every Scene: How can my Character's Weaknesses make things worse here? How can their Skills and Strengths save the day? Do this for every Scene as you write it. For now, you can think about this in an overall sense: How will my Character's Weaknesses make things worse in my Plot? How could their Skills and Strengths save them?

Do this for each of your Main Characters. You want them to truly self-sabotage because, folks, that's what we all do in real life. People don't like to grow and change. They don't like to face their fears. So it's very likely your Conflict-avoidant Character will turn away from a fight instead of leap in right away. He might do that for 90 percent of the book, creating all kinds of problems.

> The more you know about your Character's character, essentially, the more you can predict how they will react in a Scene and what the Impact of that reaction will be on the Plot.

Suggested Videos for More

BRILLIANT IDEAS I HAVE TO WRITE DOWN

THE EXTERNAL PLOT

While they can have a lot of things done *to* them in the beginning (Ruth Ware's *Zero Days* is a great example of that), they must act to get out of that predicament (which Ruth's Character does in that book). We want to read about people who act—not people who get acted upon.

If you're hearing readers or editors saying "this book is too passive" or the Characters are "passive," what that means is that you're writing a Perils of Pauline type thing where this poor victim is having all kinds of bad things happen and never, ever doing anything to get herself out of the situation.

Frankly, we hate people like that. You know, the friend who complains about how he hates his job, his dog, his yard, his furniture, his lunch. You're sitting there thinking, *Then do something about it!*

Those are not Characters we like to read about. We want Characters who act, who fight for what they want, who deserve the happy ending you're going to deliver. They can't be people who do nothing and get everything.

The #1 Thing to Understand about Plots

There's a big difference between the External Plot and the Internal Plot, and you definitely need to know both because both are necessary to have a story. Here's the big difference you need to know:

> The External plot is all the physical, tangible events and things in your book. The External Goal is something that the character can physically see, touch, hear, feel, or tangibly quantify, like finding a murderer, landing a job, or divvying up Grandpa Joe's estate. It is NOT emotional.

Everything to do with the External Plot is physical and tangible. These are actions the Character takes instead of sitting on their couch, whining and crying. They investigate the robbery, interview the bad guy, unearth the documents. They do *stuff* to get themselves out of the predicament that the Catalyst threw them into.

The External Plot is entirely about actions and stuff. Not emotions. I know, I'm repeating myself, but sometimes people get them confused. I did for a long time when I first started writing. Because I was completely missing the second kind of plot: the Internal Plot.

> The Internal Plot is all about emotion. Emotion is what binds a reader to the story. It's what they can relate to. It's how they see themselves in your Character. It is the key to an unforgettable book. It is even more vital than all the car chases and bad guys because emotion is what connects readers to your book.

You need both an Internal and External Plot to have a book that moves, that creates tension in the reader's gut (that whole "Will it work out?" feeling you want them to have). They're both worried about the Character going to meet the bad guy down a dark alley and the Character having a nervous breakdown about being in an enclosed space. They are constantly worried about the Character because every Scene presents some kind of challenge to the Character. Something to overcome.

So they can…grow and change. There, I said it again. I'll probably say it another time or ten.

Both of these kinds of Plots are made up of three parts:

> **The Goal:** What the Character wants to do/achieve/get
>
> **The Motivation:** The reason why the Character wants to do this
>
> **The Conflict:** All the roadblocks in your Character's way.

This GMC (Goal, Motivation, and Conflict) is the key to everything in your book. It is, essentially, the entire structure, which is why you need it.

If you're struggling with this, think about what fears/doubts/emotional needs you have. Great fiction is written from your gut, not your head, so get in tune with the real you to find your real Character. The Main Character doesn't have to be like you, but if you can develop an inner understanding of your Main Character's emotional story, you will create a deeper, richer story.

Let's talk about the three main components of the External Plot, how they work, and why you need them.

A GOOD IDEA TO DO

The External Goal

 This is a really, really Good Idea to Do because frankly, things have to happen in the book or the reader is going to get bored very quickly. Your Characters needs to be *active,* meaning they are actively working toward getting their way out of the Trouble that has showed up in their lives.

The Character has to have a Goal, plain and simple, because otherwise nothing happens in the book. There is no objective to achieve, nothing taking the Character from A to B.

A book is a snapshot in time in a Character's life, and there has to be a reason why you, as the author, are showing that particular snapshot.

The Goal should be difficult to achieve, and should *force the Character to grow and change* throughout the book. The External Goal is physical and tangible, remember, so it's going to be an actual thing/place/person the Character has to achieve/get.

Where to Start

Go back to the World Before the Book Starts section and remind yourself where your Character is at in his/her life. What is their Ordinary World like? Where are they living, what are they dealing with, what is their job, how do they feel about their life?

If you haven't already, write a paragraph on where they are *before the book starts*. What worries they have, what concerns they have, and what is most important in their life right then.

_____
_____
_____
_____
_____
_____
_____
_____
_____
_____
_____

Then flip back to where the Catalyst happens: This, remember, is the Trouble/Inciting Incident that sets the book in motion. It is the event that makes the Character take a turn in their life. In simple terms, it is the event that forces them to *act* (whether they want to or not, but we'll get to that Why in a second).

What event changes the trajectory of the Character's life at the beginning of the book? A murder? A divorce? An alien invasion? Whatever the Trouble is, it *must be a catalyst for change*.

_____
_____
_____
_____

_____
_____
_____
_____
_____

Now, let's use those two things to create the External Goal! How do you do that? It's easy, truly. Basically, whatever problem has been dropped into your Character's life becomes their book-length Goal. Maybe it's to catch a killer or find a lost child.

Whatever it is, it must take several steps to achieve, steps where things can go wrong, because that will make it beefy enough to carry a whole book. This is the External Goal, so it has to be a physical, tangible thing (a killer is physical and tangible, as is a lost child. Finding forgiveness is emotional so it doesn't work here…but hold onto that thought for the next section).

What External Goal has this Trouble created for the Character? If you have multiple Main Characters and/or a Villain, answer these questions for them, too.

Character 1:_____

_____

Character 2:_____

_____

The Villain/Antagonist:_____

_____

> Make sure you are only thinking about/planning the External Goal right now. These, again, are physical, tangible, quantifiable. They are not emotional. Saving the world is an External Goal. Getting a new job is an External Goal. Finding a missing loved one is an External Goal. Making amends with the past is not; it's emotional and thus, Internal, so save that one for later. :)

Suggested Videos for More

Little Scene Break

Before we move onto Motivations and Conflicts, I want you to start thinking about possible Scenes. This helps you begin to see the framework of your book, and as you plan out the External Motivations, External Conflicts, and then the Internal Plot, you should be able to see how those will affect the Scenes you are planning.

Scenes work pretty simply. They are the jigsaw puzzle the Character must put together in order to achieve their Goal. In *Taken,* Liam Neeson has to fly across the world, track down the cab driver, get info, find the hotel room, get an interpreter, find the bad guys…he has literally dozens of steps to take before he can find his daughter.

These become Scenes, and like an interlocking puzzle, they form the connection throughout your book. By planning this, you avoid having throwaway Scenes that don't advance the Plot. Scenes that don't feed into the Goal in some way don't need to be there because the cardinal rule of fiction is that:

> Every single word should advance the Plot somehow. Raise the stakes, increase the tension, and most of all, keep the reader hooked!

With all that in mind, list 10 steps your Character would need to take to accomplish their External Goal:

1. _____

2. _____ 3.

4. _____

5. _____

6. _____

7. _____

8. _____

9. _____

10. _____

You can have more, but ten is a nice number to start with because it gives you a direction. If you look at a Plot chart, you see the Scenes (steps to achieve the Goal) make the action rise (meaning become more tense). Think of it like a roller coaster: all that Tension you feel as the coaster goes up, up, up that clackety track.

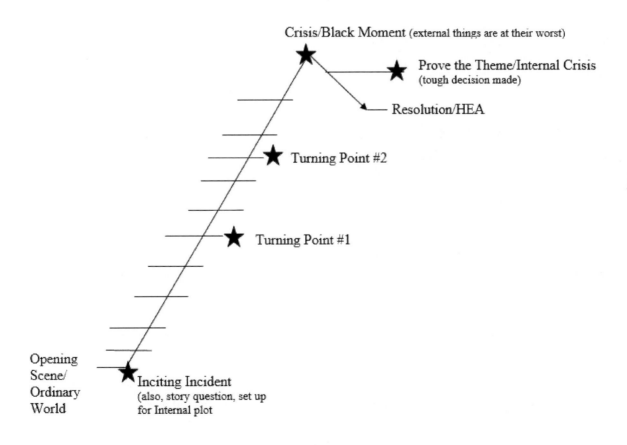

Whoo-hoo! Now you have a Goal and several possible Scenes planned for your book! You can also start thinking about Turning Points, which are places in your Plot where things go in a new direction (a great way to add more Conflict!). Let's start going deeper into your plot!

A GOOD IDEA TO DO

The External Motivation

This is another Good Idea to do. If you've ever watched a movie like *Nightmare on Elm Street,* then you are probably way too familiar with the TSTL (Too Stupid to Live) Character who goes into the abandoned building in the middle of the night for no apparent reason and gets murdered. People hate that. They want the Characters to have reasons for what they do. Those reasons are called the Motivation.

> Your Character should have a Motivation for everything they do, every move they make. It's your job, as the author, to know and understand that Motivation.

Again, we are only dealing with External Motivation right now, not Internal (although some Internal will probably leak in; you'll see).

The Motivation, essentially, is the WHY or BECAUSE. Why does Shrek want his swamp back? *Because* he likes his privacy. He's gotten pretty content in his mud-bath ogre life and *because* he doesn't want a bunch of strangers eating his food and *because* he doesn't want them sleeping in his bed, he has a reason to act. Those are External Motivations (again, External is physical and tangible, like his food and his bed). Those motivations now give him really important reasons for going to Duloc to get his swamp back. Your Character needs some, too.

What is your Character's Motivation? Why does your Character absolutely have to achieve this Goal? (If you have multiple Main Characters and/or a Villain, answer these questions for them too).

Try to list 6 Motivations. The first 2-4 reasons will likely be External, which is great. That's the kind of answer you want. The last couple of answers will probably be emotional (for example: the only place Shrek feels safe from harm and hurt is in his swamp) and that's awesome. Save those for when we do Internal Goal, Motivation, and Conflict.

1. _____

2. _____

3. _____

4. _____

5. _____

6. _____

If you are struggling with this, then I want you to answer two questions
(which are actually great questions to answer anyway):

Why has this Trouble/Catalyst come into your Character's life? Did they do anything to bring about this Catalyst for change?

_____

_____

_____

_____

_____

_____

What impact has the Catalyst had on your Character? Remember, the two most important questions you can ask in planning your book are Why and What was the Impact (watch my videos for more on that topic).

_____

_____

_____

_____

_____

Now, take a second look at those reasons why (AKA the Motivations) the Characters wants to achieve that Goal.

How will these Motivations require the Character to step outside their comfort zone (for Shrek, he has to go into town and face all the people who want to stab him with a pitchfork)?

_____

_____

_____

_____

Save this info for later! It's a great way to add depth to your Character and to your Scenes.

A GOOD IDEA TO DO

The External Conflict

Nobody likes Conflict, right? We all want peaceful, easy lives. Well, in case you haven't noticed by now, life doesn't work that way, and neither do books. Conflict is roadblocks—it's the things the Character has to overcome in order to achieve their Goal. When the Character has to work hard for their Goal, we cheer them on even more. (If all you had to do to become an Eagle Scout was buy a badge on Amazon, it wouldn't be that impressive. It's the obstacles that make it worth the ride.)

Conflict is what keeps the reader glued to the page, wondering if it will work out.

Conflict is what keeps them flipping the pages to see how on earth your Character is going to get out of that predicament.

In other words, Conflict is *crucial.*

One of the best tips I ever learned (and changed the way I wrote) is this:

> There should be Conflict on every single page of the book (external or internal).

So take some time to really think about this part of your Plot. You're going to need Conflict throughout the book to keep the reader intrigued and invested. Remember, every single page needs some.

Conflict is, like I said, all of the roadblocks that get in the Character's way. You want lots of those because if you make it too easy, the reader isn't invested in the outcome. A car ride with a lot of detours and alligators blocking the highway and storms to outrun…that's far more interesting than the same commute you have every day. People care about the first story and get bored with the second.

The External Conflict is also called the BUT. Shrek can get his swamp back, BUT he has to go rescue the princess. He can bring the princess back, BUT she wants a kiss. He wants to marry her, BUT she's already marrying Lord Farquaad.

Those Conflicts are all obstacles he must overcome in order to achieve his Goal of getting his swamp back (and being loved for who he is, but that's an emotional thing, so save that for the Internal Plot).

Here's another example: In *Pretty Woman,* Edward has to buy a business from a businessman who doesn't want to sell. He also has to find a no-strings date, deal with Stuckey, etc. His Goal of buying the business, continuing his world domination plan, and getting out of town is completely thrown out the window when he meets Vivian. Everything he tries to do faces an obstacle of some kind. Sit down and analyze that movie (or any movie you really love), and list out the obstacles, AKA the Conflicts, that the Character has to overcome.

Your Character needs *lots* of these to keep the book moving along at a good clip, keep the reader's interest, and most of all, raise the stakes. That means that things keep getting worse and worse for your Character because the minute things are wonderful and awesome, the reader loses interest. To them, the book is done when everyone is happy and safe. Keep the reader on their toes!

List 6 potential External Conflicts your Character will face in their quest for their External Goal:

1. _____

2. _____

3. _____

4. _____

5. _____

6. _____

Bonus Question: Why will your Character force themselves to battle or overcome these obstacles? This is an emotional thing, so if you don't have it yet, no problem! You'll discover it in the Internal Plot section.

_____

_____

_____

_____

_____

_____

_____

_____

You know what that answer just gave you? More Motivation for your Character!

Writing the GMC Statement

Now, let's put it all together into a single sentence that you can hang over your computer monitor to remind you what the core of your book is about. I find that having this one sentence helps me keep everything on track and keeps me from adding unnecessary Scenes. In fact, I used to hang this sentence (and the one you will do in the next section) up every time I started a book to make sure I stayed on track with every page!

This simple but powerful sentence is the framework for your book, and the simpler you can make it, the easier it is to stick to it. Do one for each of your Main Characters and your Villain, if you have one:

_____[MainCharacter]_____ wants _____[External Goal]_____

because_____[Motivation]_____but _____[Conflicts]_____get in the way.

Suggested Videos for More

BRILLIANT IDEAS I HAVE TO WRITE DOWN

THE INTERNAL PLOT

First, a little refresher:

> The Internal Plot is all about emotion. Emotion is what binds a reader to the story. It's what they can relate to. It's how they see themselves in your Character. It is the key to an unforgettable book. It is even more vital than all the car chases and bad guys because emotion is what connects readers to your book.

Here's the thing you might not know about the Internal Plot: often, the Character has *no idea* what his/her Internal Goal, Motivation, and Conflict are because by and large, most of us don't go around thinking about our emotional needs. I don't know about you, but I think about what my stomach needs A LOT more often than what my heart needs!

Maybe if we go to therapy, we do, but otherwise, most of us are just trying to get through the day. We don't dwell on our emotional journey or our past traumas or our insecurities. Neither do your Characters, unless those thoughts are *triggered* by an event.

> Emotions, thoughts, Character histories should all be triggered by Plot events. Something happens, and that makes the Character think about a past event or present issue.

I have a video that shows you exactly how that trigger works and how to use it in your book: https://youtu.be/n2mWOYboqOU

A GOOD IDEA TO DO

The Internal Goal

This is a really, really Good Idea to Do because even if the Character is *unaware* of their Internal Goal, all major Characters in the book must have one (back to that whole emotional bond thing with the reader). You absolutely need the reader to bond if you want them to stick with the book.

Think of your book like a new puppy. You want readers to love it so much, they can't imagine a second apart from it. They swear up and down to walk it, feed it, care for it…

Oh wait, that was my kids with our dog. But you want the reader to do the same thing and not get bored in the first few chapters and forget the book exists. That's the kiss of death to your story.

We read books and relate to the Characters because we connect to what they are going through emotionally. We see Characters who are like us or like people we know. They have our fears, anxieties, insecurities. The External Plot may be something we would never experience ourselves (as much as you might want to be a Jason Statham-type assassin, chances are none of us will be), but the *emotional* journey should be something that we either could imagine going through or have gone through. Those feelings of not being enough, not being up to the challenge, not feeling secure, etc. We connect with the feelings, not the car chases.

> ### SUPER IMPORTANT THING TO REMEMBER:
> Readers bond with your Characters because of emotional connections, not car chases.

We also read books to see the Characters grow and change, to evolve into better beings who deserve the happy ending the author is giving them. The bad news is…they can't do that without confronting and dealing with their issues.

That's the case in real life, too. We hate those people that get everything they ever wished for without working for it. Or the narcissist who marries up and into royalty. That kinda irks us. But when the people we know fought for what they have, well, we're right there with some pom-poms and champagne, cheering them to the finish line.

Think about it like this: We all have that insecure friend who chooses a Mr. Wrong. No matter how many red flags she sees, she's convinced that this Mr. Wrong will be THE ONE. They have a toxic relationship, break up, get back together, rinse and repeat, until she moves on to the next Mr. Wrong, and the next one. You're on the sidelines thinking, *Honey, deal with your issues and get your act together.*

And maybe you gift her a free session on BetterHelp.com for Christmas! Just kidding. Sort of.

Your Characters are the same. Their Internal Goals are emotional and are caused by Deep Emotional Wounds, which we talked about earlier (which is why figuring those out is a Good Idea, too).

We all have Deep Emotional Wounds, which cause traumas, anxieties, insecurities, unresolved issues, fears, and more. Your friend who falls in love with Red Flag Guy every time definitely had something happen to her when she was younger that caused her to have attachment and insecurity issues. Maybe Mom and Dad had a bitter divorce, or maybe she was abandoned as a kid. Whatever issues she has, they *manifest in her reactions and actions later in life.*

That's how the Internal Plot works. The stuff that caused those emotional issues is going to make your Character react and act in a certain way to the events the Plot throws at them. A person with abandonment issues is going to react and act differently than a person with self-esteem issues.

Whatever Deep Emotional Wounds your Characters have will also form the basis of the Internal Goal. Like the External Goal, the Internal Goal should be difficult to achieve and should *force the Character to grow and change* throughout the book.

> Remember, the Internal Goal is not at all like the External Goal. Internal is entirely emotional. It won't involve a car chase or a promotion or a flower garden or even a puppy. It will be all about the Character's Internal emotional arc and either resolving or healing their Deep Emotional Wounds.

Go back a few pages and take a look at those Deep Emotional Wounds that your Main Character has.

Think about how those issues will make your Main Character feel, act, and react, right this minute. How will they react to rejection? Loss? Solitude? Failure? Success? Love?

_____

_____

_____

_____

_____

_____

_____

_____

Then, if you haven't already, I want you to write a paragraph on where they are EMOTIONALLY before the book starts. What secrets are they hiding? What fears do they have? What self-blame/self-hatred do they feel? How are they insecure/traumatized/anxious, and most of all, WHY do they have these issues? (We love Why and What Was the Impact!)

_____

_____

_____

_____

_____

_____

_____

_____

_____

How the Catalyst ALSO Creates the Internal Goal

Another little refresher, in case you skipped those pages: The Catalyst is what sets the book in motion. It is the Inciting Incident/event that makes the Character take a turn in their life. The Catalyst that sets off the

Internal Plot can be (and often is) the same as for the External Plot. The difference? This Catalyst will *force your Character to confront their deepest fears and anxieties.*

When Liam Neeson's daughter is kidnapped in *Taken*, it sets off all those insecurities and doubts he had about himself as a father. He knows he wasn't there when his family needed him—because they've left him/divorced him over it. He thinks he can repair that relationship when wham, his daughter is kidnapped because she didn't open up to him enough to share the truth about her trip to Paris. Nothing like feeling like a parental failure on two continents, am I right?

What event changes the trajectory of the Character's life at the beginning of the book? A murder? A divorce? An alien invasion? Whatever the Catalyst is, it must set off a change. What does this Catalyst do to your Character emotionally? Is it going to make them face their deepest fears?

_____

_____

_____

_____

_____

_____

This answer becomes the basis of the Internal Goal because the Catalyst has changed *everything* for the Main Character. Wherever they thought they were going/whatever they thought they were doing next is forever changed because of the trouble that came into their lives at the beginning of the book. For example: John McClane's wife being kidnapped at the beginning of *Die Hard*. That is the Catalyst that detours his attempt to repair his relationship with her (his emotional Internal Goal) because deep down inside, he knows he has not been there for his family all these years.

Take a second and think about that Internal Journey for your Main Character and how it relates to the External Plot. In *Taken*, Liam Neeson's Internal Goal is to repair his damaged relationship with his daughter. That's pretty obvious when he shows up at the house, hoping to spend time with her and give her a gift. This rift between them was caused by the Deep Emotional Wounds he created by not being there for his family. He probably has a few Deep Emotional Wounds himself around abandonment and self-reliance.

So how is he going to accomplish his Internal Goal of repairing that damaged relationship?

I'll give you a second. Don't skip ahead. Think about it. Because when you learn how to pick these out on your own from what you see and read, it makes figuring it out for yourself a LOT easier.

(insert *Jeopardy!* music)

Ding, ding, ding: Liam Neeson is going to accomplish his Internal Goal of repairing the damaged relationship with his daughter through his actions in the External Plot! He is going to be there for his family by physically rescuing his kidnapped daughter. Great, we love action like that! But we also want emotion. (Remember, emotion binds the reader, not car chases).

> Did you just see how it all ties together? I get so excited when I figure that out. One Plot impacts the other, impacts back, impacts again, like dominos. That creates Rising Stakes where the Goal gets more important with every single Scene.

Once Liam Neeson has done all that hero stuff to rescue her and accomplished his External Goal, he has the mental/emotional space to accomplish his Internal Goal. Literally, his daughter is there, in the flesh, and it's his chance to *finally* repair those bonds. He has proved his love with his actions, now he's gotta match that with some words of love. We know they have some repairing yet to go, but there is hope that they will become a happy father/daughter again.

I love it when a story all ties together!

Now it's your turn to figure out your Character's Internal Goal. This might be tough for you. Lots and lots of writers (myself included) struggle with this.

It's hard to know your Character's deep down emotional needs. It's so much easier to know the External than the Internal. But it's there; I guarantee it. Look back at their Deep Emotional Wounds if you need some clues to the Internal Goal.

What is the emotional, *deep-down-in-their-soul* thing the MC wants and needs to achieve before the end of the book. *What do they want deep down inside and, most of all, emotionally?* Be loved for who he is, ogreness and all (*Shrek*), repair his relationships (*Die Hard*), be loved for who he is and as he is (Edward in *Pretty Woman*), etc.? This goal should take SEVERAL steps to accomplish. What is your Main Character's Internal Goal?

_____

_____

_____

_____

_____

_____

_____

_____

_____

Deep Emotional Wounds (DEW) are the key to everything. If you haven't figured out your Main Character's DEW, do that now. In the movies I mentioned, the DEWs are present in scenes like when Edward talking about his father with Vivian in the bathtub. His relationship with his father is a DEW that still pains him. Edward has spent his whole life trying to prove he is something to others when really he needed someone who saw beneath the money and success. Enter Vivian.

In this section, make sure you are only thinking about/planning the Internal Goal. These, again, are emotional and caused by past traumas.

The Internal Goal is all about healing of some kind. What emotional scars does your Character need to heal? Don't worry about _how_ exactly they're going to do that. We'll get to that in a minute.

Remember, the Internal Goal should require many, many steps to make it happen (because we don't just get over our hurts and hangups overnight or by magic, hence why there are twelve-step programs, because we all know it takes work to become a better human), but they work differently than External Goals a little bit.

Here's another cool tidbit that creates a more compelling book: _Internal Goals are interconnected with every single action the Character takes._ Which means when the Character takes an action, it is somehow touching on his Internal Goal and forcing him/her to grow and change/conquer a fear/overcome an insecurity, or fail and then confront their inner demons.

Don't believe me? Go back and analyze every Scene in _Taken_. How did Liam Neeson have to face his Deep Emotional Wounds and his Internal Goal in each Scene? He tries to find her and fails, over and over again. What does that do to his Internal Goal?

When you don't have that interconnectivity between actions->reactions->emotional demons, the book will read flat or feel disconnected. That's why taking some time to work on this—okay, a lot of time—is so, so, so crucial.

Every physical action the Character takes in the book should intertwine with their Internal Goal because their actions awaken their deepest fears, cause them to see themselves in a new light, or expose their inner doubts and insecurities. These actions bring them closer and closer to the things they fear most about themselves.

Let's talk about my perpetually favorite movie, the one I put on when I'm sick because it always makes me smile: *Pretty Woman.* In that movie, Richard Gere's Character, Edward, has lots of actions that are designed to push Vivian away emotionally. He keeps his guard up, doesn't get close. She does the same thing by refusing to kiss him on the mouth…until she falls in love and kisses him when she thinks he's sleeping. She's taking a risk that could get her rejected, but she's still afraid that he doesn't love her, which is why she does it when he's sleeping.

Edward is just as terrified of rejection, even if he doesn't seem it. Why does Edward send Vivian home at the end? Because he still doubts that he can be loved for who he is, as he is. It is only when he finally accepts himself, warts and all, and overcomes his fears (metaphorically and physically, by climbing the ladder) that he finds true love and gets his act together enough to propose.

Let's dive a little deeper into *Taken* and see how this plays out in the Scenes. When Liam Neeson goes to his ex's house with a gift for his daughter at the very beginning, it's an olive branch of sorts. That's his first action toward his Internal Goal of repairing his family bonds. But…she's been kidnapped, and so what does that cause inside of him emotionally?

Guilt. Self-recrimination.

And a drive for revenge to hurt the people who took her. Ooh, all nice emotional things! It also reinforces his Internal demons (Deep Emotional Wounds) about *not being there when his family needed him.*

Look at every action he takes: tracking down the cab driver (who dies before Liam gets all the info, another failure and reason to multiply his guilt), meeting with his colleague (who is murdered by the bad guys; yet another person that Liam has not only let down but also *not been there to take care of*), rescuing the wrong girl (failure of a kind and a possibility his daughter is dead and thus, he has failed her entirely).

He has literally *dozens* of steps to take before he can find his daughter. And every single one of them makes him confront his worst fear—that he is too late to fix things.

These actions become Scenes, and like an interlocking puzzle, they create the rising stakes of the External—physical—story (things keep getting worse for poor Liam's daughter) and for the *emotional* story, the Internal Plot.

The action (rescuing the wrong girl) leads to a reaction (I saved someone, but it's not my daughter; I have failed her yet again) which leads to an emotional impact (he again has let her down and this time, his failure may mean she is dead, the ultimate letdown for his family). See how the emotional stakes get higher for Liam as the physical stakes do?

All this creates that oh-so-vital reader connection throughout your book. By planning this kind of interlocking jigsaw-puzzle Plot wizardry, you avoid having throwaway Scenes that don't advance the Plot. Scenes that don't feed into the Internal Goal in some way don't need to be there because the cardinal rule of fiction is that:

> Every single word should advance the Plot somehow. Raise the stakes, increase the tension, and most of all, keep the reader hooked!

Yeah, I said that earlier. I might even say it again. Live with it. It's an important concept.

With all that in mind, go back to Part 1 where you listed 10 steps your Character would need to take to accomplish their External Goal. Now, I want you to list 10 *emotional ramifications* if those steps go awry or the Character fails.

1. _____

2. _____

3. _____

4. _____

5. _____

6. _____

7. _____

8. _____

9. _____

10. _____

Failure, in a book, is *great*. Like I said, nobody likes the kid that gets all As, becomes the All-Star of the basketball team, gets into every college they apply to, inherits a million dollars from Grandpa…

We like the underdogs, the people who overcome setback after setback to succeed. Seeing the janitor with cancer who won the Powerball on the news? That made me choke up! The guy who was already a retired millionaire who won it…I clicked away and didn't care.

If you plan on having the Character succeed in some of these Scenes, note what insecurity/emotional issue that moment awakens. For instance, Shrek succeeds in rescuing the princess, but then realizes she thinks he's some charming prince and he wants to hide his ogre/always-rejected self from her. This feeds into his inner fears that being an ogre means no one wants him or will ever love him.

How will these Scenes awaken/trigger your Character's insecurities or anxieties or inner fears?

1. _____

2. _____

3. _____

4. _____

5. _____

6. _____

7. _____

8. _____

9. _____

10. _____

Remember in the Plot chart, the Scenes (steps to achieve the Goal) make the action rise (meaning become more tense). The two Plots—External and Internal—are both doing that. Not necessarily at the same pace, but they should both have rising stakes. Here's another secret:

> As the External Plot stakes get higher with each Scene, so too do the Internal Plot stakes. The Character should be continually forced to grow and change even more with every single Scene.

Here's that Plot chart again so you can see what I mean. See it this time through the lens of the emotional Internal Plot:

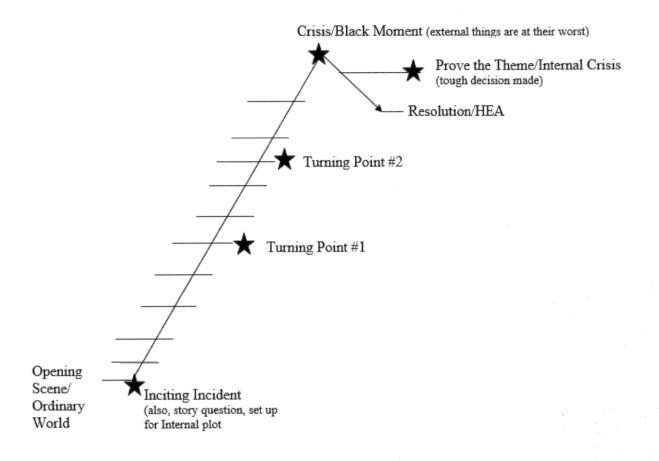

If you're having trouble seeing that, map it out for a pretty clear plot movie, like *Taken* or *Shrek*. Write out the Scene action and emotional ramification on the Main Character for each Scene. You'll see pretty quickly how the stakes rise.

_____

_____

_____

_____

_____

A great book is like a roller coaster that keeps getting more and more tense before you have the relief of the falling action (the ending of the book). That's the feeling you want your reader to have. That is accomplished with the emotional connection because the reader is so fully invested in what happens to the Character.

Try analyzing movies or books you love every time you watch them/read them (I do this sometimes and it drives my husband crazy). Name the External Goal, Motivation, and Conflict, then the Internal Goal, Motivation, and Conflict for the Main Character.

With each Scene, make a note of what action the Main Character took and how it affected the External Plot (pissed off the bad guy, exposed his position to the enemy, left him stranded on an island, etc.).

Now, write down how that action affected the Main Character emotionally (meaning Internally).

Did it make him afraid to antagonize the bad guy again, make him terrified that he will get his friends killed, leave him afraid that he will never get back in time to save his family, or an even bigger emotion—*leave him doubting himself and his ability to save them?*

Look for doubts, insecurities, anxieties. Those are GREAT Internal elements!

I even made you a handy-dandy chart.

External Action	External Affect	Internal Action	Internal Affect

> Don't worry about piling on the emotional stakes. People don't grow and change unless they are forced to by the circumstances around them.

The reader *wants* to see the Character struggle, suffer setbacks, and deal with the ramifications of their DEWs, their actions, and their choices. Kinda like watching your kids struggle to pay the rent because they spent all their money going to Coachella. It's hard to do, but so much growth for the kid if you let them struggle and learn.

A GOOD IDEA TO DO

Internal Motivation

This is a pretty important thing to the book and here's why: As I said earlier, people don't change without a *reason* to change. Maybe they have hit rock bottom or their past has come back to haunt them or they have lost something that matters. Whatever life-changing moment has come into their life when the Catalyst happens is also the Catalyst for them changing and growing emotionally (whether they know it or not).

Their Internal Motivation gets them up off the couch and doing something about where they are at in life.

Think of Sigourney Weaver in the movie *Copycat*. She's an agoraphobic who has to get over her agoraphobia in order to catch a killer. People dying—and her own life and peace being threatened—is enough to force her into changing. Nothing that happened to Sigourney before this killer was on her doorstep was enough to motivate her to change. A killer in her house? Well, that's a pretty strong motivator!

Your Character should always have a Motivation for the way they act, the way they react, and the choices they make. We all have Motivations for everything we do, even if we don't realize it. I wander into the kitchen because I want a snack or it's time to cook dinner. I take a walk with the dog because I want to see what the new neighbors are up to (and tire out the dog). I sit down at my computer because I want to write. There's a Motivation behind every single action everyone—including your Characters—takes.

The Motivation, as we've talked about before, is the WHY or BECAUSE. The Character needs to achieve a Goal (Shrek wants to get his swamp back so he can be alone again) for a reason. That's the Motivation—and while there are External reasons for this (the fairytale creatures are eating his food and sleeping in his bed), there should also be *emotional* reasons behind this Goal. Those are the Internal Motivations.

So, from an *emotional* standpoint, why does Shrek want his swamp back (his Internal Goal)?

Because the people in Duloc hate him, taunt him, try to stab him. Deep down inside, he's easily hurt and just wants other people to love him. That's his Internal Motivation.

Remember the sentence you created in the External GMC plan? That's going to apply to Internal as well:

> **The Character wants what (the Goal) because (the Motivation) but (Conflict) gets in his/her way.**

Don't worry about writing it now. We'll get to it in a second.

Think deeply about this part of your book because Motivation is the key to believability. You can make *anything* work if it is properly motivated.

You can literally make a Character kill his own grandmother—if it's a choice between Granny and his own child. That's a Motivation (a sad one!). Look at movies like *The Box, Sophie's Choice,* and *Of Mice and Men* to see that in action.

It's the same with the Internal Motivation. You can make revenge a great Internal Goal if the revenge your Character seeks is deeply motivated. Maybe he wants to get revenge against the people who left him bankrupt, resulting in him and his mother living on the streets. She died in the cold because she was homeless. Seeing her suffer because of another Character's actions gives your Main Character a lot of Motivation for wanting revenge.

The Motivation has to be strong, believable, and rooted in those Deep Emotional Wounds I keep talking about.

For your Main Character(s): Why *emotionally* does your Character need to achieve this Goal? I want you to list three reasons why (you might have come up with some of these in the External Plot plan Motivation exercise).

1. _____

2. _____

3. _____

If you are struggling with this, then I want you to answer this question:

What impact has the Deep Emotional Wound that is driving their Internal Goal had on your Character? In other words, how have their past hurts made them into the people they are today and why?

_____

_____

_____

_____

_____

_____

Remember, the two most important questions you can ask in planning your book are Why and What was the Impact (watch my videos for more on that topic because I talk about it a lot).

Once you have these Motivations, I want you to take a second look at them and see if they are strong enough to make your Character step outside their comfort zone (Shrek will risk possible imprisonment in Duloc and his life because he is so deeply motivated emotionally to avoid hurt).

Do any of them need tweaking/tightening?

1._____

2._____

3._____

Just as you did with the External Plot, I also want you to look at things that are outside your Character's control that are having an impact on them *emotionally*. Like with Shrek, Donkey's undying devotion makes him risk a little and open up. He can't control Donkey, no matter how hard he tries, and the impact on Shrek is a slow and gradual opening up to his friend. Then Fiona's "rejection" makes him withdraw and not tell her how he feels.

Can you name a few of these moments for your Character?

1._____

2._____

3._____

PRO TIP:

Study the movies and shows that you love. Figure out the Character's Deep Emotional Wounds in their past and how those are impacting their emotional reactions and growth.

A GOOD IDEA TO DO

Internal Conflict: The Key to Reader Love

I mentioned this before, but I'm going to say it again because it was such a great lesson: *Conflict must be on every single page of the book (External or Internal).* Conflict is, as I said earlier, all of the roadblocks, and in the case of Internal Conflict, those roadblocks can come from their own fears, anxieties, insecurities, as well as other Characters.

Remember all those issues you figured out before? Well, they create conflicting emotions in your Character.

Include LOTS of these because you want the reader to root for your Character's success. We love people who battle impossible odds to find true love or get home or deliver the ring to the mountain. Readers love, love, love to see that happen, *especially when the Character has to overcome a whole lot of self-doubt, insecurity, anxiety, and other fears to do it.*

That is Internal Conflict. And that is what you want to write a lot of in your book because it makes the reader your Character's biggest cheerleader.

The Internal Conflict is the BUT, just like with External Conflict, except the Internal Conflict is all about emotions and fears. It's all those emotional things that keep your Character from growing and changing. The "buts" that get in the way of them dealing with their issues.

For Shrek, one of his Internal Conflicts is Fiona's interpretation of what a hero should look like. He doesn't look like that and so he is terrified of rejection when she asks to kiss her knight in shining armor. That fear is the BUT that keeps him from kissing her.

For Edward in *Pretty Woman,* it's the feelings he starts developing for the owner of the business. He becomes torn about what he is going to do to that owner, and even as we see him pursuing moves like stalling the Navy contracts, he is wrestling with his emotions over the right thing to do. With Vivian, he has a literal two-roads moment in front of the elevator. Does he ask her to stay and confess his love or does he let her go?

In other words, does the Character open up and be who they deep down want to be or do they keep themselves walled off/not change? That is what you want for your Character. Trust me, readers LOVE IT.

List 6 potential Internal Conflicts your Character will face during the book:

1. _____

2 . _____

3. _____

4. _____

5. _____

6. _____

Why will your Character force themselves to battle or overcome emotionally in your book?

_____

_____

_____

_____

_____

You know what that answer just gave you? More Motivation for your Character! Motivation is all those Why answers, and when the Motivation is strong enough, the Character will do whatever it takes to succeed at their goal.

Now, let's put it all together into a single sentence that you can hang over your computer monitor to remind you what the core of your book is about. I find that having this one sentence helps me keep everything on track and keeps me from adding unnecessary Scenes. Remember, this sentence is ONLY for the Internal Plot (you already have one for the External Plot, so this one should be all about the emotional journey of the Character):

_____ [MainCharacter] _____ wants _____ [Internal Goal] _____

because_____ [Internal Motivation] _____ but _____ [Internal Conflicts] _____get

in the way.

Now What?

Now we are going to tie it all together! And, you know, write the book. Planning is all well and good, but you gotta write it for people to read it. Just sayin'.

To get started with the next step, ask yourself one key question:

What life lesson/message do you want your Reader to take from your book?

Meaning, what lesson is your Character demonstrating? For instance: Seeking revenge can destroy all the good in your life. Or…being afraid to be yourself costs you the happiness you want. Or…shutting yourself off from people will make them leave anyway. Something like that.

Figure that out, put those two External and Internal Plot sentences together, and you will have an entire Plot for your book!

Suggested Videos for More

BRILLIANT IDEAS I HAVE TO WRITE DOWN

BRILLIANT IDEAS I HAVE TO WRITE DOWN

GOING DEEPER WITH YOUR BOOK

We're not going to delve too deeply into this part, ha ha, because I want you to master creating an amazing Plot before throwing a whole lot of other things into it. Not that you can't—in fact, some of the best books have the two things I'm going to talk about here—but just know the rules of the road before you start taking wild detours.

Plot Twists

To create Plot Twists, you want to think about how things could go wrong. Like really, really, really, really wrong. A lot of times when I start reading a book and I see a Plot point come up, I start trying to figure out the most twisty way the author could have written that before I get to the answer. I was reading a book where the Main Character had a memory of blood being on the floor. I went through a whole list of things that could have happened in the past and came up with some pretty interesting murder theories that may or may not have happened in the book (spoiler alert, my conspiracy theory answer wasn't right, but it did give me an idea for a story!). It's just fun to see how else you would write a Scene!

Let's face it: a smooth ride is not interesting to read. The reader wants to see the Character struggle and suffer setbacks. The more things go awry, the more fun the ride will be!

Remember that list of Scenes you wrote? Now, I want you to list 10 possible things that could go wrong during the 10 steps above. These can also become Conflicts (the roadblocks in your Character's way) or Turning Points, as you saw in the Plot chart.

1. _____

2. _____

3. _____

4. _____

5. _____

6. _____

7. _____

8. _____

9. _____

10. _____

Impossible Choices

To make it a little deeper, let's shoot for some Impossible Choices. Like when Darth Vader tells Luke Skywalker that he's his father—whoa, what a Conflict that created! Does he still kill him, knowing this? Impossible Choices are the *Tale of Two Cities* type situation where the Character either confesses his identity and faces certain death or takes the death penalty because of his deep love for another Character. I love Impossible Choices, but you can't always work one into your book. But if you want to try, do this:

List three potential Impossible Choices (seemingly insurmountable Conflicts) for your Character:

1. _____

2. _____

3. _____

Going Deeper with the Characters

The best thing to do to go deeper with your Character is research human behavior. I read a lot of self-help books over the past few years and learned a lot about birth order, attachment theory, mental health, substance abuse disorders…and how that all ties in together.

It not only helps you figure out the Why behind your Character's actions, but it makes you super-fun at parties (ha ha, just kidding) when you analyze your friends! No, don't do that. They don't like it. Trust me on that one.

I'm not going to do a lot of exercises here because I could write a whole 'nother book just about Character-writing exercises, but these ones should help you dig a little deeper:

What is your Character's deepest fear? What are they most afraid of losing?

Who is your Character closest to in their life? If it's a friend, why a friend and not a family member? If it's a family member, why that particular family member? And why are they not close to the other members of their family?

Is your Character the oldest, middle, youngest, or an only child? How did that birth order impact them growing up? Did it make them more/less responsible? More/less spoiled?

What is your Character like in a relationship? Do they keep their emotional cards close to the vest? Do they get insecure? Do they always fear the worst? Or do they dive right in with their whole heart? Why or why not?

There is a whole lot more we can delve into for Characters. I do that in some of my videos and include writing exercises sometimes, so check out all those handy-dandy QR codes I peppered throughout this book for you.

All that said, the best way to get to know your Characters, see if your Plot works, and actually become a better writer is to…

Write.

Don't put it off. Don't get trapped in "analysis paralysis" where you are constantly researching and planning instead of writing.

> Nothing teaches you more about writing than actually writing.

If you're feeling lonely in your writing quest, check out the live streams on the channel. I'd love to see you and write with you—and talk more writing!

Now finish that book so voracious readers can dive into your amazing creation!

Suggested Videos for More

BRILLIANT IDEAS I HAVE TO WRITE DOWN

FAQ

Do I plan out the Plot first or the Characters first?

Honestly, I sort of do both. As you can see in the workbook, a lot of who the Character is has a bearing on the Plot, and vice versa. You have to know who is in your book and how you are going to make them face their worst fears. But that said, you do you. No writer has exactly the same writing process, so do what works for you. There are no rules!

How do I set a writing schedule?

First, make it a priority to yourself. I know what it's like to have no one support your dream, and I spent years getting up at 4:30 in the morning to write before anyone woke up. I'd stay up late at night, writing some more. I wanted to be an author so badly that I found the time. I kept notebooks with me and wrote in them when I had a few minutes before a doctor's appointment or in the carpool lane. Find the time that works for you and stick to it. Because your voice deserves to be heard.

How do I know if I have enough of an idea for a whole book?

The basic rule of thumb is whether it takes a lot of steps to accomplish. You don't have to have everything in this workbook figured out or filled out before you start writing. You just have to have a Goal that is big enough to require a lot of steps and important enough to the Character that they will embark on that journey.

What is the number-one mistake I could be making?

Not watching my channel! Ha, just kidding. Not really. The biggest mistake I see is a lack of an Internal Plot. I know because I was the poster child for that. Watch the videos where I analyze Scenes and see how the Internal Plot is interwoven. Too many authors want to be too nice to their Characters, and that means they aren't forced to face their fears, grow and change. That will make a book drag and will make the reader disconnect.

How do I learn to move on from Chapter One?

For every chapter, you have to keep writing. Seriously. You are going to hit a snag at Chapter Two or Chapter Fifteen or Chapter Twenty. Go back to the chapter before, and ask yourself: How *can I make things so much worse for my Character here? What is the last thing the reader would expect? What will put them in a really scary/emotionally vulnerable position?* And then do that to the Character for the next chapter!

How do I learn more? How do I get better at writing?

Read, read, read and write, write, write. You can't become an author if you don't read because reading gives you an innate sense of structure. And you definitely can't become an author if you don't write. Nobody gets to the Major Leagues overnight. They did it by studying everything they could and practicing over and over and over again. That's how people become authors, too. They don't just grow on trees.

What if I think I can't do it? What if I suck? What if I can't write? What if...

Listen, you're *always* going to have those thoughts. We all have them, no matter where we are at on the career totem pole. The fact that you are reading this workbook and investing time and energy into improving your story and your writing is evidence that *you can and should write.*

Yes, you might (okay, probably) will suck when you first start out. I sure did. Check out this video that analyzes my very first manuscript (https://youtu.be/6Ido69_qyjY?si=njMsS6Z7VWqwDcJU). It's all part of the process. Remember what I said about the Major Leagues? Do you think Mookie Betts caught the first ball thrown to him at second base? Or the hundredth? He caught some, but not all, and he probably would tell you that he messed up more than he succeeded, especially in the beginning. But he kept showing up at practice, kept throwing and catching, kept learning from the pros, and kept going. That's how he got to the Dodgers. He wasn't dropped onto the field by a fairy godmother. He worked his butt off.

You're going to have to do that too if you want to write an outstanding book. Even after all I have published, I am driven to make the next book better than the last book. I always feel like that last book wasn't my best and I can do better. That's what keeps me showing up at the keyboard, reading the best authors, and working my butt off.

I'll leave you with the quote that got me through all those years of rejections (ten books in eight years; I have the box of rejections to prove it):

> "It's a dreadful shame how many wonderful books we will not be able to read because someone gave up their dream too soon."
>
> SUE-ELLEN WELFONDER

Keep writing, my friends. Just keep on writing.

Shirley

ABOUT THE AUTHOR

Shirley Jump, author of *Writing Compelling Fiction,* is an award-winning, *New York Times, Wall Street Journal,* Amazon, and *USA Today* bestselling author who has published more than 80 books in 24 countries, that have sold more than 8 million copies. She has spoken all over the world about the power of narrative and how to create compelling books. A former reporter and communications director for a marketing agency, she uses her diverse background to help clients create impactful books that readers can't down.

She knows the path to publication isn't all rainbows and unicorns, so to help writers write their best possible book, she offers monthly Manuscript Masterminds through her website, WritingCompellingFiction.com. On her channel, YouTube.com/@WritingCompellingFiction, she unlocks the secrets behind compelling novels and delves into the psychological aspect of overcoming creativity-stoppers like doubt and perfectionism. Follow her channel for more writing exercises, classes, and behind-the-scenes writing lessons or join her Manuscript Mastermind to build your tribe of like-minded writers and receive crucial feedback on your pages. If you have a writing question you'd like to see answered, email her at: Shirley@WritingCompellingFiction.com.

BRILLIANT IDEAS I HAVE TO WRITE DOWN

BRILLIANT IDEAS I HAVE TO WRITE DOWN

BRILLIANT IDEAS I HAVE TO WRITE DOWN